our pact

This is a special journal between only us. We agree (and pinkie promise swear) that anything we write in this book will not be discussed with, or shown to, anyone else.

Signed by:

Mom:

Me:

ISBN: 978-1-963674-34-7

Printed in the USA

Love
BETWEEN
a mother
AND SON IS
forever

Mother and Son Journal

A Pass Back and Forth Between You and Me Journal

how to use this journal

Before you start, sit down with your mom and talk about how you want to use this journal. We've included some ideas below, but if you want to adjust them, just take a pen and mark them up - this is your journal, so take charge!

If you want to create new rules, we've left some space for you to write your own at the bottom.

First, choose a page to complete - it doesn't have to be in any particular order, pick any one you like.

On some pages there will be sections for you to fill-in, and others for your mom. Simply complete your part and leave the "mom" ones for her (we've marked them with this fancy star so you know they're for mom...she's pretty fancy, right?)

After you've completed a page, mark it with one of the accompanying bookmarks so your mom knows where to look, and how urgently she needs to respond (she'll have her own set and do the same):
Red urgent
Yellow would love to hear back sooner than later
Green no rush

Choose a designated spot to leave the journal for the other person once you are finished. It could be under their pillow, in their sock drawer,
on their desk, or any other secret spot.
Our secret exchange spot will be:

Be open. The more you're willing to share, the more you will get out of the journal.

Additional "Rules":

Want to talk more? If after writing you want to talk face-to-face about something, let your mom know so you can find a time to sit down and discuss further. You can even make up a secret code word if you feel like something's on your mind, but don't know how to start the conversation. Drop the code word and you can have a talk as soon as possible.
Our secret code word is:

our bucket list

Let's make a list of 10 things we want to do together before I graduate from high school.

mom's top 10

1. ______________________
2. ______________________
3. ______________________
4. ______________________
5. ______________________
6. ______________________
7. ______________________
8. ______________________
9. ______________________
10! ______________________

my top 10

1. ______________________
2. ______________________
3. ______________________
4. ______________________
5. ______________________
6. ______________________
7. ______________________
8. ______________________
9. ______________________
10! ______________________

Circle the ones you like best on the other person's list. Pick which one(s) you can do this year and create a plan to make it happen:

____

____

____

____

things i love

5 things mom loves about me

1. ______________________________
2. ______________________________
3. ______________________________
4. ______________________________
5. ______________________________

5 things I love about my mom

1. ______________________________
2. ______________________________
3. ______________________________
4. ______________________________
5. ______________________________

favorite things

These are a few of our favorite things...

	mom ✪	me
Favorite TV show:		
Favorite song:		
Favorite meal:		
Favorite color:		
Favorite vacation:		
Favorite sleeping position:		
Favorite friend(s):		
Favorite teacher:		
Favorite thing to do when I need "alone" time:		
Favorite thing in my room:		
Favorite game to play outside:		
Favorite game to play inside:		

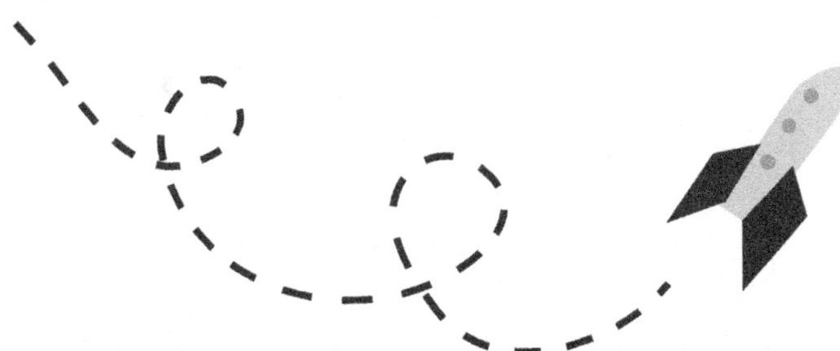

if I could go anywhere in the world...

mom

I would go here:

I'd be with:

I would do these things there:

me

I would go here:

I'd be with:

I would do these things there:

this or that For Mom

Success ❄ Happiness

Apathy ❄ Obsession

Skill ❄ Popularity

Poor And Happy ❄ Rich and Miserable

Cherished ❄ Respected

Hero ❄ Antiher

happy Ending ❄ Sad Ending

this or that
For Me

Success ❄ Happiness

Apathy ❄ Obsession

Skill ❄ Popularity

Poor And Happy ❄ Rich and Miserable

Cherished ❄ Respected

Hero ❄ Antiher

happy Ending ❄ Sad Ending

ten quick questions

	mom ✪	me
Last person who made me laugh:	___	___
Song that is stuck in my head:	___	___
I will never, ever, ever eat:	___	___
Outfit that is currently on repeat:	___	___
Last thing I ate:	___	___
Best day of the week:	___	___
Best time of the day:	___	___
I cannot live without my:	___	___
When I am sad, this makes me feel better:	___	___
My favorite subject at school is/was:	___	___

would you rather...

	mom ✪	me
build a snowman or a sand castle?		
it be Halloween or Easter?		
be able to fly or be invisible?		
ride a bike or ride a camel?		
be an eagle or a cheetah?		
be really strong or really fast?		
swim in the ocean or in a pool?		
only be able to whisper or to yell?		
be too hot or be too cold?		
be able to breathe underwater or read people's minds?		
live in a big city or a small town?		
spend the night camping or in a hotel?		
eat ice cream or cake?		

three wishes

If I had three wishes,

I would wish for these things:

mom's wishes

for me:

___

___

___

for my family:

___

___

___

for the world:

___

___

___

my wishes

for myself:

___

___

___

for my family:

___

___

___

for the world:

___

___

___

If I had a free day to do whatever I wanted, I would...

mom ✪

me

If I could be invisible I would...

mom ✪

me

What do you do during a typical day when I’m at school?

mom ✪

Here’s what I do during a typical day at school:

me

If we switched roles for a day, I'd be most excited to do this:

mom ✪

me

And least excited about:

mom ✪

me

I think we're really similar because...

mom ✪

me

I think we're different because...

mom ✪

me

My favorite things to talk to you about are:

mom ✪	me

I find it really hard to talk to you about:

mom ✪	me

You make me feel special when...

mom ✪

me

When you were my age, what did you like to do?

mom ✪

If I were a grown-up I'd do these things differently:

me

Some things that worry me are...

me
answer here

thoughts/questions on the answer above

Some things that worry me are...

answer here

me

thoughts/questions on the answer above

Sometimes I can't sleep because I'm thinking about...

me
answer here

mom
thoughts/questions on the answer above

Sometimes I can't sleep because I'm thinking about...

answer here

me

thoughts/questions on the answer above

I wish I could do this with you more...

me
answer here

mom 
thoughts/questions on the answer above

I wish I could do this with you more...

answer here

me

thoughts/questions on the answer above

I wish you'd help me more with...

me

answer here

mom ✪

thoughts/questions on the answer above

I wish you'd help me more with...

answer here

me

thoughts/questions on the answer above

I feel the most loved when...

me

answer here

mom ✪

thoughts/questions on the answer above

I feel the most loved when...

mom ✪

answer here

me

thoughts/questions on the answer above

I wish I knew how to...

me

answer here

thoughts/questions on the answer above

I wish
I knew how to...

answer here

me

thoughts/questions on the answer above

I wish people knew these things about me:

me
answer here

mom ✪
thoughts/questions on the answer above

I wish people knew these things about me:

answer here

me

thoughts/questions on the answer above

Someone was mean to me because they did/ said this:

me

answer here

My reaction was:

It made me feel:

thoughts/questions on the answer above

Someone was mean to me because they did/ said this:

answer here

My reaction was:

It made me feel:

me

thoughts/questions on the answer above

I felt so proud of myself when...

me
answer here

thoughts/questions on the answer above

I felt so proud of myself when...

answer here

me

thoughts/questions on the answer above

I get nervous when...

me

answer here

thoughts/questions on the answer above

I get nervous when...

mom ✪

answer here

me

thoughts/questions on the answer above

Today I just want to complain about...

me

answer here

thoughts/questions on the answer above

Today I just want to complain about...

answer here

me

thoughts/questions on the answer above

The worst thing happened at school/work/home today...

me
answer here

mom ✪
thoughts/questions on the answer above

The worst thing happened at school/work/home today...

answer here

me

thoughts/questions on the answer above

I just have to get this off my chest...

me

answer here

thoughts/questions on the answer above

I just have to get this off my chest...

answer here

me

thoughts/questions on the answer above

Today I want to tell you something that's been on my mind...

me
answer here

thoughts/questions on the answer above

Today I want to tell you something that's been on my mind...

answer here

me

thoughts/questions on the answer above

The most embarrassing thing that's ever happened to me is...

me
answer here

thoughts/questions on the answer above

The most embarrassing thing that's ever happened to me is...

answer here

me

thoughts/questions on the answer above

When I grow up I want to be...

me
answer here

mom ✪
thoughts/questions on the answer above

When I grow up I want to be...

answer here

me

thoughts/questions on the answer above

Mom, I have a question for you:

(write your question below)

respond here

Mom, I have a question for you:

child's name

(write your question below)

me

respond here

Drawing Pages

Draw a picture of your child **– make sure to include lots of details and labels!**

me

Draw a picture of your mom **– make sure to include lots of details and labels!**

drawing pages

Start drawing a picture, but don't finish! Pass it on and have the other person complete it.

drawing pages

Draw a picture of your dream vacation

mom ✪

me

drawing pages

Draw how you feel today

mom ✪ me

drawing pages

Draw a picture of how you would give your room a make-over. Include lots of details and labels!

mom's room ✪

my room

drawing pages

Draw a picture of yourself as a super hero. What's your super power?

mom ✪

me

drawing pages

Draw yourself in your most favorite place in your house

drawing pages

Think about your upcoming birthday. Draw a picture and write about what you want to do on your birthday or for your birthday party. Who's there? What does your cake look like? Where would you go?

mom ✪

me

drawing pages

What would your "best day ever" look like? Draw a picture and explain.

mom ✪

me

Where would you go? Who would you be with?

drawing pages

Draw what it feels like to be:

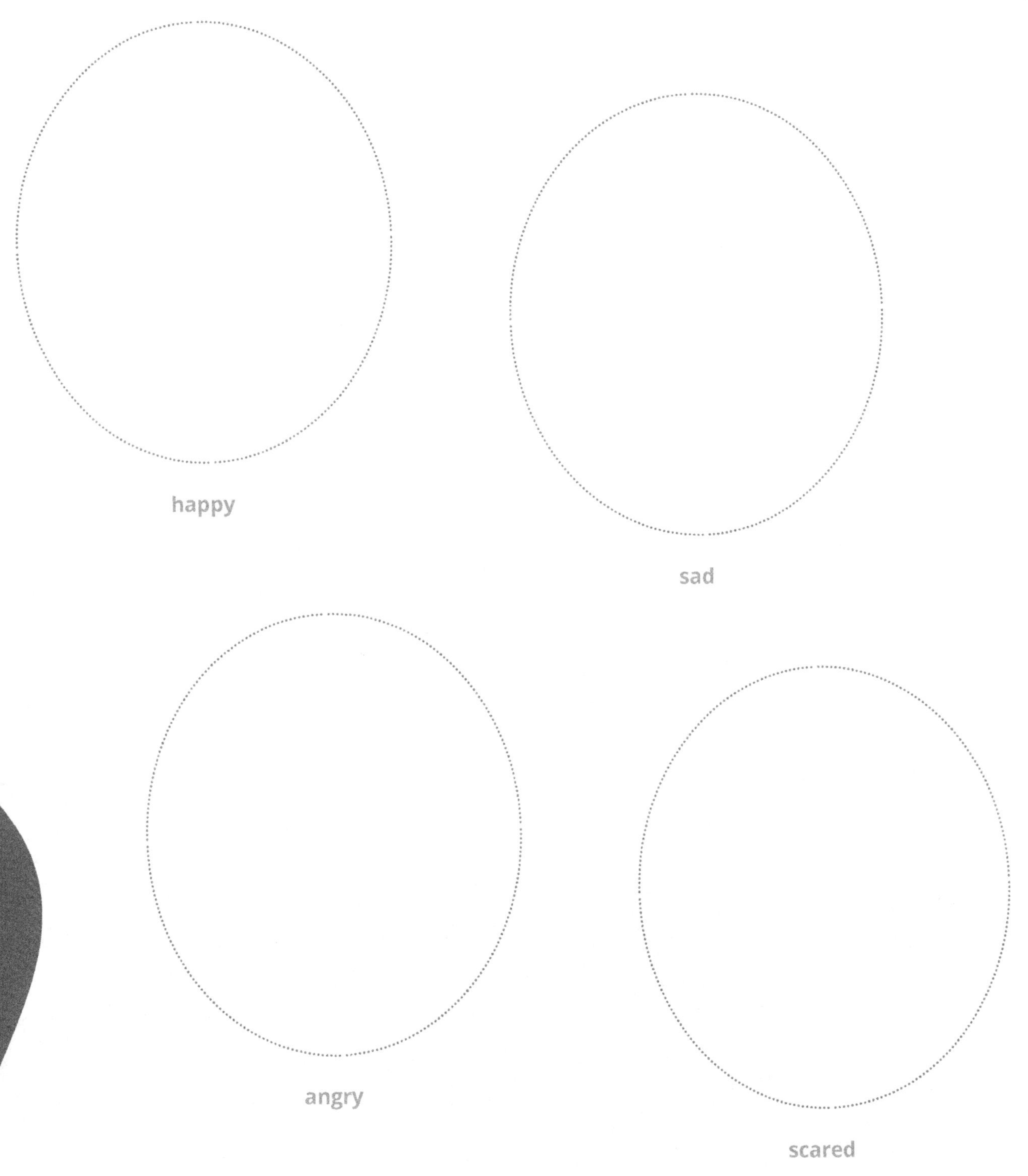

use these extra pages if you need more space for a response

use these extra pages if you need more space for a response

bookmarks for me

Cut out these bookmarks and after you've completed a page in the journal, place one of them inside so the other person knows where to look, and how urgently they need to respond.

bookmarks for mom

Cut out these bookmarks and after you've completed a page in the journal, place one of them inside so the other person knows where to look, and how urgently they need to respond.

Made in United States
North Haven, CT
04 May 2024

52105693R00039